# THE THIRTEEN COLONIES

## A TRUE BOOK

by

**Brendan January**

**Children's Press**®
A Division of Scholastic Inc.

New York  Toronto  London  Auckland  Sydney
Mexico City  New Delhi  Hong Kong
Danbury, Connecticut

Colonists hard at work building their new community

*The photo on the cover and the title page depicts Jamestown, Virginia, in 1615.*

Library of Congress Cataloging-in-Publication Data

January, Brendan, 1972–
    The thirteen colonies / by Brendan January.
        p. cm — (A True book)
    Includes bibliographical references and index.
    Summary: Examines the creation of the original thirteen colonies in the United States, from the failed colony of Roanoke in 1587 to the formation of the Georgia colony in 1733.
    ISBN 0-516-21631-7 (lib. bdg.)    0-516-27197-0 (pbk.)
    1. United States—History—Colonial period, ca. 1600–1775—Juvenile literature. [1. United States—History—Colonial period, ca. 1600–1775.] 1. Title. II. Series.
E188 .J36  2000
973.2—dc21                                                      00-022591

11 12 13 14 R 11 10 09 08 07 06 05

# Contents

The First Communities   5

The New England Colonies   12

The Middle Colonies   21

The Southern Colonies   31

European to American   40

To Find Out More   44

Important Words   46

Index   47

Meet the Author   48

Replicas of the three English ships—*Godspeed*, *Discovery*, and *Susan Constant*—which brought the colonists to Jamestown in 1607.

# The First Communities

On December 16, 1606, three ships loaded with food, tools, and 105 men left London, England. These brave men were sailing to North America. The people of Europe (a region made up of many different lands, including England, France, Italy, and Spain) had known of the land since Columbus sailed in 1492.

In 1587, the English had built a colony in North Carolina called Roanoke. But when ships visited again in 1590, they found that everyone had mysteriously vanished.

Now, the English were trying again. This time, they planned to build a city on the coast of what we today call Virginia.

After four months at sea, the travelers joyously sighted land in April 1607. They sailed up a

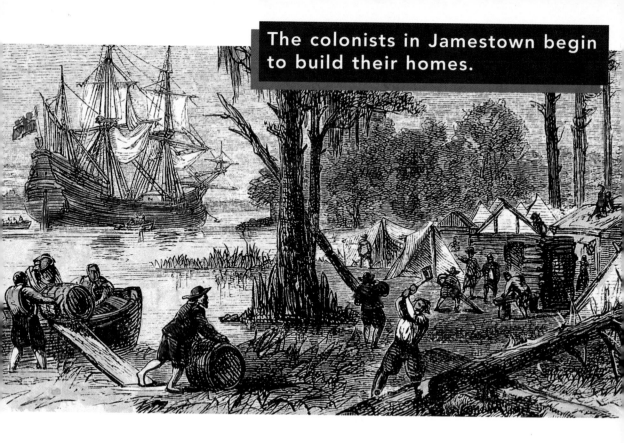

The colonists in Jamestown begin to build their homes.

river that they named after their king—the James River. About 60 miles (97 kilometers) from the coast, they founded a community called Jamestown. While living in a new land, the people still considered their town a part, or colony, of England. They followed the same customs and obeyed the same laws as they had back in England.

The men hoped to find gold and precious metals in America. Instead, supplies ran out. The desperate colonists traded iron tools for corn from American Indians. In autumn 1609, five hundred colonists lived in Jamestown. By the next spring, only sixty had survived.

Captain John Smith helped to save the Jamestown colonists from starvation by trading with American Indians for food.

Help arrived from England in June 1610, and the colony grew stronger. The Indians looked at Jamestown with growing anger and fear. The Europeans were moving onto their hunting

Tension over land grew between the colonists and American Indians.

LOSSING- BARRITT.

grounds. The Indians attacked the town, but they could not defeat the Englishmen, who were armed with guns.

In England, another group of colonists sailed for Virginia. They called themselves Pilgrims.

On September 16, 1620, 102 Pilgrim men, women, and children boarded a ship, the *Mayflower*, and began their voyage. But a fierce storm blew them off course. Instead of finding Virginia, the Pilgrims landed off Cape Cod in Massachusetts.

The Pilgrims' ship, the *Mayflower*, arrives in Plymouth Harbor.

# The New England Colonies

Unlike the colonists in Virginia, the Pilgrims did not seek gold or riches. They came to America in search of freedom to practice their religion. The Pilgrims, called Puritans, hoped to establish a pure and holy land. "We shall be as a city

The Pilgrims

upon a hill," wrote a Pilgrim leader. In 1620, they built a tiny village called Plymouth.

More Puritans arrived shortly after the Pilgrims, also looking for religious freedom in the new land. The Puritans were strict and hardworking. They spread out into New England, clearing forests and plowing the rocky soil. In each community, the Puritans built their houses around the church and the watchful eye of the minister.

But protests erupted. As more colonists came to New England, they grew tired of the Puritans' harsh laws. A minister named Roger Williams

Roger Williams, founder of Rhode Island

disagreed with the Puritan Church, and in 1636, the Puritan leaders ordered him to leave. Williams traveled south and founded a new colony, Rhode Island.

To the north of Massachusetts, another colony had been formed in 1623—New Hampshire. The early colonists lived by trading furs and catching fish. New Hampshire's trees were especially valuable. An Englishman traveled every winter into the land's thick forests. He marked tall pine or oak trees to be cut down. They were then dragged to the coast and used as masts for British war ships. Later, these trees would be used to build ships for American whalers and fishermen.

Other English colonists began traveling south and west in search of valuable furs. In 1638, a group of Puritans established a colony called Connecticut.

Connecticut had some of the best farmland in New England. The Connecticut colonists seized

Corn growing on a Connecticut farm

land deep in American Indian territory. The Indians watched with growing frustration and rage. By 1675, more than fifty thousand colonists were living in New England.

Metacomet, the chief of the Wampanoag tribe, plotted revenge. He urged other American Indians to rise up and drive the colonists back into the sea. In 1675, Metacomet led raids against New England towns.

Hundreds of colonists and American Indians died in the

terrible fighting. Twelve New England towns were completely destroyed. But the Indians did not have enough men and weapons. They began to surrender. Those who did not surrender were

Metacomet, leader of the Wampanoag tribe, was killed by colonial soldiers.

killed or captured. In August 1676, Metacomet was killed and the war ended. The colonists called Metacomet Philip. Today, the conflict is remembered as King Philip's War.

# The Middle Colonies

While the English Puritans settled New England, other colonists were moving to the land between New England and Virginia. These territories became the middle colonies—New York, Pennsylvania, Maryland, and Delaware.

New York was first settled by the Dutch. In 1626, the Dutch

Peter Minuit bought Manhattan Island for the Dutch in 1626.

governor bought Manhattan Island for $24 worth of beads and jewelry. The Dutch then built a city on the island and named it New Amsterdam after the capital of their homeland.

The Dutch colonists also moved into the Hudson River

Valley. They divided the land into giant farms called estates.

In August 1664, an English fleet of war ships appeared in New Amsterdam Harbor. The English demanded that the Dutch surrender. The Dutch

New Amsterdam Harbor during the 1660s (left) and the same area today, called New York Harbor (below)

had little choice. The English king gave the colony to his brother, James, the duke of York. The colony was renamed New York in his honor.

The duke of York also organized an area to the west of New York and called it New Jersey. The rulers in New Jersey hoped to attract colonists. They offered free land and said that newcomers could worship as they pleased. Many different kinds of people flooded into New

James, the duke of York, later became king of England in 1685.

Jersey—Puritans from New England and Quakers from England, Ireland, Scotland, and Wales.

To the west of New Jersey was a powerful and rich colony called Pennsylvania. Named after Admiral William Penn, the colony was founded by the admiral's son, also named William.

Penn belonged to a religious group called the Quakers. They were called "Quakers" because they often shook with joy during their meetings.

The Quakers, like the Puritans, wanted to build a home for themselves and their beliefs. Penn planned a capital city for the colony called Philadelphia, which means "city of brotherly love."

William Penn, the founder of Pennsylvania

Penn hoped that all people in the colony would live together in peace.

Thousands of Quakers moved to Pennsylvania in the late 1600s. The soil was fertile and the colonists thrived. The Quakers

William Penn and other Quakers meet with their American Indian neighbors.

also became known for their honesty. They paid fair prices for land from American Indians. Of all the colonists, only the Quakers were trusted by American Indians.

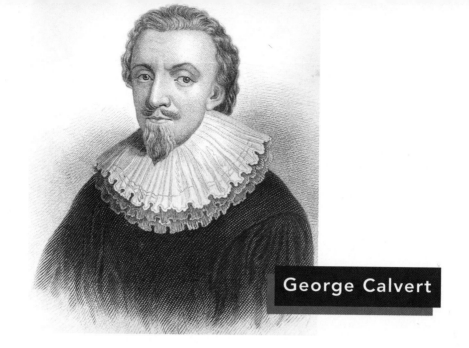

George Calvert

In 1632, King Charles I gave land north of the Potomac River to George Calvert, a Roman Catholic, His sons started the colony of Maryland in 1634. The Catholics, like the Puritans and the Quakers, were hated in England. Free to practice their

Local Maryland officials planning the layout of Baltimore

religion, Catholics settled in Maryland in large numbers.

The Delaware Colony was first known as New Sweden. The Swedish newcomers established the colony in 1638, but lost it to the British in 1664. In 1776, the colony officially became Delaware.

# The Southern Colonies

By 1650, Jamestown had become a part of Virginia, the largest and most powerful colony in the South. Rich landowners cleared forests and planted tobacco. The landowners were desperate for workers. They sent letters to England, begging people

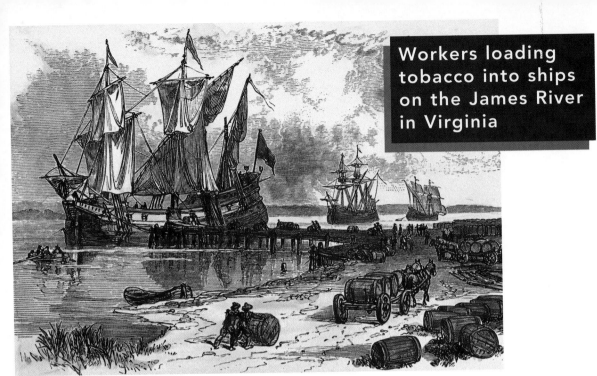

Workers loading tobacco into ships on the James River in Virginia

to come. Virginia, they wrote, had plenty of food and work. Many Englishmen responded. Between 1620 and 1642, more than eighty thousand people made the voyage from England to North America.

Many of the travelers could not pay for the trip, and so they became indentured servants. Indentured servants had to work for a period of time—from five to twelve years—after they arrived. Then they were free.

In 1619, Europeans began shipping slaves from Africa to Virginia. At first, landowners set the Africans free after several years of work. But they needed workers to harvest huge fields

Slaves from Africa arriving in Jamestown

of tobacco. White farmers started to keep black workers for their entire lives. They also made the black workers' children serve them too. This is how slavery began in North America.

# Virginian Leaders

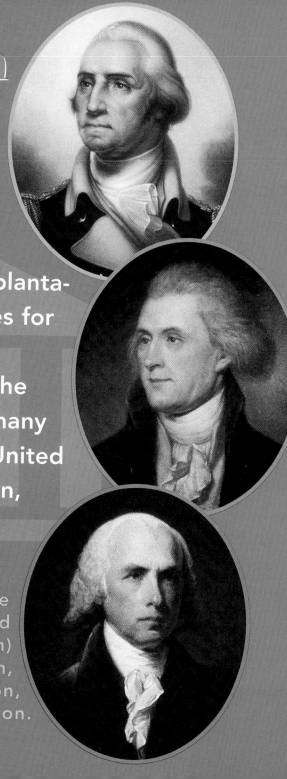

By the 1700s, a wealthy class of landowners had appeared in Virginia. They owned giant farms called plantations and relied upon slaves for work. They also held high positions in government. The Virginia colony produced many of the first leaders of the United States—George Washington, Thomas Jefferson, and James Madison.

Famous residents of the Virginia Colony included (from top to bottom) President George Washington, President Thomas Jefferson, and President James Madison.

Farmers planting crops in the South Carolina Colony

Many Virginians and north-ern colonists moved south in search of new land. Originally part of the same colony, North and South Carolina were officially divided into separate colonies in 1712. Tobacco did not grow well in the Carolinas. Instead, colonists planted rice and indigo, a plant used to dye cloth a rich purple color. Charles Town (now Charleston) in South Carolina became the largest city in the southern colonies.

Georgia became a colony in 1733. The leaders of Georgia

wanted a place for the poor of England to live. Many English people were locked in prison because they could not pay their debts. In Georgia, they had a chance for a new life.

At first, everyone in Georgia owned a small farm. They were forbidden to sell land or own slaves. But this system failed. No one could clear and farm enough land alone. By 1750, slavery was legal and land could be bought and sold

A slave child living in a small cabin by fields of crops

in Georgia. By 1776, almost forty thousand colonists lived in Georgia. Half of them were slaves.

# European to American

By 1750, the English colonies had become vibrant and strong. More than one million colonists lived in cities and on farms from Georgia to New Hampshire. Most of the colonists still lived close to the sea. Cities like Philadelphia, New York, and Charleston became important centers of trade.

In the next twenty-five years, an amazing change took place. Europeans from Germany, England, Scotland, and Holland

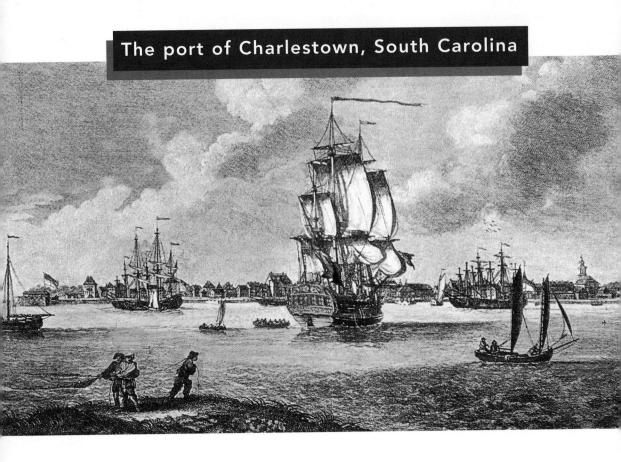

The port of Charlestown, South Carolina

began to think of themselves as Virginians, New Yorkers, and New Englanders. The European colonists were becoming Americans.

# Colonial Population

**B**etween 1700 and 1770, the population of the colonies exploded, from 251,000 in 1700 to almost 2,100,000 in 1770.

| | 1700 | 1770 |
|---|---|---|
| Connecticut | 26,000 | 183,900 |
| Delaware | 2,500 | 35,500 |
| Georgia | N.A. | 23,400 |
| Maryland | 29,600 | 202,600 |
| Massachusetts | 55,900 | 235,300 |
| New Hampshire | 5,000 | 62,000 |
| New Jersey | 14,000 | 117,400 |
| New York | 19,100 | 162,900 |
| North Carolina | 10,700 | 197,200 |
| Pennsylvania | 18,000 | 240,100 |
| Rhode Island | 5,900 | 58,200 |
| South Carolina | 5,700 | 124,200 |
| Virginia | 58,600 | 447,000 |

*There are no numbers available for Georgia for 1700 since the area became a colony in 1733.*

# To Find Out More

Here are some additional resources to help you learn more about the thirteen colonies:

 **Books**

Doherty, Kieran. **Puritans, Pilgrims, and Merchants: Founders of the Northeast Colonies.** Oliver Press, 1998.

Hakim, Joy. **Making Thirteen Colonies.** Oxford University Press, 1993.

Smith, Carter, ed. **The Arts and Sciences: A Sourcebook on Colonial America.** Millbrook Press, 1994.

Smith, Carter, ed. **The Explorers and Settlers: A Sourcebook on Colonial America.** Millbrook Press, 1994.

# Organizations and Online Sites

### Archiving Early America
*http://earlyamerica.com/*

A site that provides insight into diaries, letters, and newspapers written in colonial times.

### Colonial Almanac
*http://www.history.org/ almanack.htm*

The "Historical Almanack" allows you learn about colonial life, important colonial figures, and see historic places.

### Colonial Williamsburg Foundation
P. O. Box 1776
Williamsburg, VA
23187-1776
*http://www.history.org/*

### Plimoth Plantation
P.O. Box 1620
Plymouth, MA 02362
*http://www.plimoth.org/*

### Virtual Jamestown
*http://jefferson.village. virginia.edu/vcdh/ jamestown/*

As part of the four hundred-year anniversary of Jamestown, this site offers a tour of the village and discusses its importance in history.

# Important Words

*colony* group of people who leave their native land to settle in another land but still obey the laws of the mother country

*conflict* struggle, battle or war

*Europe* region made up of many different lands, including England, France, Germany, Holland, Italy, and Spain

*fertile* able to support and nourish crops

*indentured servant* person who signs a contract to work for another for several years and cannot leave

*Pilgrims* group of people who came to North America in 1620 seeking religious freedom and built the community of Plymouth in Massachusetts

*Puritans* group of people who came to North America shortly after the Pilgrims and were also seeking religious freedom

*thrive* to grow strong and rich

# Index

(**Boldface** page numbers indicate illustrations.)

American Indians, 8–10, **9, 10,** 18, 20, **20,** 28, **28**
Calvert, George, 29, **29**
Catholics, 29, 30
Charleston, 37, 40, **42**
conflict, 10, 18–20
Connecticut, 17, **17,** 43
Delaware, 21, 30, 43
duke of York, 24, **25**
Europe, 5, 40–42
Georgia, 37–39, 40, 43
Jamestown, **4,** 7–9, **7, 9,** 31, 34
Jefferson, Thomas, 35, **35**
Madison, James, 35, **35**
Manhattan, 22, **22**
Maryland, 21, 29–30, **30,** 43
Massachusetts, 11, 16, **19,** 43
*Mayflower,* 11, **11**
New Amsterdam, 22, 23, **23, 24**

New England, 12–21, 25
New Hampshire, 16, 40, 43
New Jersey, 24–25, 43
New York, 21, **22, 23,** 24, 43
North Carolina, 6, 37, 43
Penn, William, 26–27, **27, 28**
Pennsylvania, 21, 25–27, 43
Philadelphia, 26, 40, **41**
Pilgrims, 10–13, **11, 13**
Plymouth, **11,** 13
Puritans, 12–15, 17, 21, 25, 26, 29
Quakers, 26–29, **28**
Rhode Island, 15, 43
slaves, 33–35, **34,** 38, 39, **39**
Smith, John, **9**
South Carolina, **36,** 37, 43
Virginia, 6, 10, 12, 21, 31–35, 43
Washington, George, 35, **35**
Williams, Roger, 14–15, **15**

# Meet the Author

Brendan January was born and raised in Pleasantville, New York. He attended Haverford College in Pennsylvania, where he earned his B.A. in History and English. He earned his master's degree at Columbia Graduate School of Journalism. An American history enthusiast, he has written several books for Children's Press, including *The Emancipation Proclamation*, *Fort Sumter*, *The Dred Scott Decision*, *The Lincoln-Douglas Debates*, and *The Assassination of Abraham Lincoln*. Mr. January lives in New Jersey and works as a journalist at the *Philadelphia Inquirer*.